WORLD

The journey is long and hot. You travel across dry land, with rocky hills and small trees. Then you must walk between high mountain walls. At last you begin to leave this dark place and come into the light. And suddenly you have arrived in Petra, and you can see in front of you the beautiful building of pink stone called the Treasury. You are looking at one of the world's wonders.

There are old wonders and new wonders in the world. Some are made by people, and some belong to the natural world. From these thousands of wonders, the author has taken eleven of his favourites – cities and temples, from the east and the west, from the sea, the land, and the sky. Turn the page, and come on a journey to some of the most wonderful things in the world today.

OXFORD BOOKWORMS LIBRARY

Factfiles

World Wonders

Stage 2 (700 headwords)

Factfiles Series Editor: Christine Lindop

BARNABY NEWBOLT

World Wonders

OXFORD UNIVERSITY PRESS

OXFORD
UNIVERSITY PRESS

Great Clarendon Street, Oxford OX2 6DP

Oxford University Press is a department of the University of Oxford.
It furthers the University's objective of excellence in research, scholarship,
and education by publishing worldwide in

Oxford New York

Auckland Cape Town Dar es Salaam Hong Kong Karachi
Kuala Lumpur Madrid Melbourne Mexico City Nairobi
New Delhi Shanghai Taipei Toronto

With offices in

Argentina Austria Brazil Chile Czech Republic France Greece
Guatemala Hungary Italy Japan Poland Portugal Singapore
South Korea Switzerland Thailand Turkey Ukraine Vietnam

ISBN: 978 0 19 423776 5

A complete recording of World Wonders is available
in a CD pack ISBN: 978 0 19 423779 6

Printed in China

Word count (main text): 6,738

For more information on the Oxford Bookworms Library,
visit www.oup.com/elt/bookworms

ACKNOWLEDGEMENTS

The publishers would like to thank the following for permission to reproduce images:

Cover image: Robert Harding World Imagery (Tesoro monument seen from As Siq gorge, Jordan/Cubo Images).

Map and diagram: pp.3, 30 by Peter Bull

The publishers would like to thank the following for permission to reproduce images: Alamy Images pp.0 (The Pyramids at
El Giza/nagelestock.com), 4 (As Siq gorge/CuboImages srl), 6 (Layers of sandstone/Peter de Clercq), 7 (Serengeti
National Park/LOOK Die Bildagentur der Fotografen GmbH), 9 (Crocodile/Paul Souders/World Foto), 9 (Masai
Mara Game Reserve/WorldFoto), 10 (Angkor Wat/Kees Metselaar), 12 (Angkor Wat East Gallery bas relief scene/
Wolfgang Kaehler), 15 (Iguazu Falls waterfall/Tibor Bognar), 16 (Viewing platform at the Iguassu Falls/South
America), 17 (Pyramid of Kukulcan/Jordi Cami), 19 (The Sacred Cenote, Chichen Itza/amjad el-geoushi),
19 (Juego de Pelota/imagebroker), 22 (The Cedar Breaks Amphitheater/Russ Bishop), 27 (Alhambra/B.O'Kane),
31 (Aurora Australis from space/ImageState), 32 (Saiho-ji garden/Lonely Planet Images), 33 (Kiyomizudera
Temple/Asia Images Group Pte Ltd), 34 (Ryoanji/John Lander), 35 (Great Barrier Reef/David Wall), 35 (St John's
Reef, Red Sea/Images & Stories), 36 (Dugong sea cow/Martin Strmiska), 37 (Turtle at Moore Reef/Lonely Planet
Images), 37 (Crown of thorns starfish/Lonely Planet Images), 40 (Xi'an, Terracotta Warriors/PCL), 40 (Terracotta
warrior soldier/Shaun Higson), 28–29 (Aurora Borealis/Jaspal Jandu); Oxford University Press pp Activity A
(Red Tail Boa Constrictor/Photodisc), Activity B (International flags/Photodisc), Activity C (Waterfall/Photodisc),
Activity D (Park/Comstock), Activity E (Dhammayangyi Temple/Photodisc), Activity F (Amazon jungle/Photodisc);
Photolibrary pp.24 (The Alhambra Palace/Robert Harding Travel), 33 (Kinkaku-ji/Robert Harding Travel); Robert
Harding World Imagery pp.5 (El Khazneh/Michael Runket), 13 (Ta Prohm temple, Cambodia/Bruno Barbier),
23 (Colorado River/Panoramic Images), 26 (Alhambra Palace/James Emmerson), 39 (Terracotta Warriors Tomb/
Cubo Images), 41 (Millau bridge/Eye Ubiquitous), 20–21 (Grand Canyon at dusk/Panoramic Images).

CONTENTS

The Great Pyramid (centre)

1   A world of wonders

Which is the tallest building in the world? Which is the oldest building? Which mountain is the highest? Perhaps you know the answers to these questions – or perhaps you do not. But each of these questions has only *one* answer. And your answer is either right or wrong.

But you can ask different questions. Which is the most beautiful building in the world? Which is the best waterfall? Which place in the world is the most wonderful? Each of us has different answers to these questions. And no one's answer is right or wrong. So why do we ask the questions? Because the world is full of wonders, and we cannot see them all. But we want to learn about them, because perhaps – one day – we will see some of them. And because we like to know that they are still there.

The Greek writer Herodotus asked himself these questions nearly two thousand years ago. He described some of the Wonders of the Old World. Today, nearly all of his Wonders have gone. Only one of his Wonders is still here. Do you know what it is?

The Wonders in the book by Herodotus were all buildings – or statues like the Colossus at Rhodes. This tall statue, more than 30 metres high, stood at the entrance to the harbour on the Greek island of Rhodes.

Another Wonder for Herodotus – his oldest Wonder, and the only Wonder from the Old World still here today

– was the Great Pyramid in Egypt. When Herodotus was alive, the Great Pyramid was already an old building, two thousand years old. And for nearly four thousand years, the Great Pyramid was the tallest building in the world.

But for us today, wonders are not all buildings. Some of them are natural – like forests, rivers, mountains, or waterfalls. These are the new wonders of the world. Of course, they are not 'new' at all. Our forests, rivers, and mountains are older than any of our buildings. For a long time – for thousands of years – some people did not think that they were wonderful. But then we started to lose them. Now we understand that the world is always changing. Buildings fall down, rivers lose their water, and forests burn.

Because of this, it is important for us to learn about the wonders of the world. If we are not careful, we will lose them. Only one of the old Wonders is still here today, after more than two thousand years.

In the next eleven chapters, you can read about some natural wonders, and some wonders that were made by people. Are they the greatest wonders in the world today? What do *you* think?

Aurora Borealis

Arctic
Ocean

Pacific
Ocean

EUROPE

Millau Bridge

Alhambra

Great Pyramid

Petra

ASIA

Kyoto

Terracotta
Army

Angkor Wat

Pacific
Ocean

Great Barrier Reef

AUSTRALIA

Indian
Ocean

N

AFRICA

Serengeti Migration

Aurora Australis

Atlantic Ocean

SOUTH
AMERICA

Iguazú Falls

NORTH
AMERICA

Grand Canyon

Chichén Itzá

Pacific
Ocean

0   2000   4000 km

World wonders in this book

2 Petra – city of pink stone

You always come to Petra from the east, and you always come on foot – or perhaps on a camel. The road to Petra is too narrow for a car. For the last two kilometres, you travel through a mountain, and the road is only five metres across. But the walls on both sides of the road are hundreds of metres high. This is the entrance to Petra, and it is called the *Siq*.

The Siq

When you visit Petra, you walk through the *Siq*. And when you come to the end of the *Siq*, you see the most beautiful building in the world. It is called the *Khazneh* (the Treasury). It is tall, and it is made of pink stone – but you can only see the front of the *Khazneh*. The rest of the building is inside the mountain. People made the building two thousand years ago, but they did not build it – they *cut* it into the mountain.

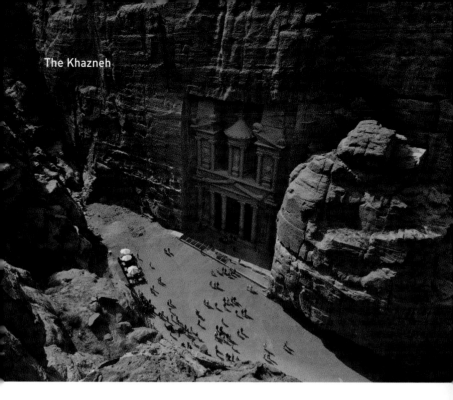

The Khazneh

About 2,500 years ago, a group of Arab people called the Nabataeans moved to south Jordan. They made their capital city at Petra, in the mountains. It was a good place for a city. First, it was good place for a market. Petra was on the old road between Egypt and Arabia (to the south) and Syria, Greece, and Rome (to the north). Travellers came along this road with things to sell, like gold and spices. Second, it was a good place to defend. The mountains around Petra were stronger than any walls. And third, there was water. The Nabataeans were very good builders. They made dams to hold the water, and long canals to move it around the city. Two thousand years ago, Petra was a rich and important city with strong, beautiful buildings, and thousands of people living there. Now no one lives there, and the city has gone. What happened?

The Nabataeans began to build Petra in about 400 BC. But then, in the year AD 363, there was a terrible earthquake, which destroyed much of the city. Two hundred years after that, in AD 551, there was another bad earthquake. People moved away from Petra, and they stopped using the road for business. They began to use ships – not camels – to carry their spices and gold. And the world forgot about Petra for more than a thousand years.

The pink stone of Petra

But Petra is still there. The earthquakes destroyed the buildings on the land, but they did not destroy the buildings in the mountains. Many of these beautiful buildings are tombs – places for dead bodies. They are empty now, but you can still visit more than 500 of them. At the far end of Petra is a tomb called the Monastery, which is 50 metres high. But it is the beautiful pink stone front of the Treasury that is in everybody's photos of Petra. At the very top of the Treasury is a stone urn (like a large stone cup). For hundreds of years, people thought that there was treasure in the urn. They shot their guns at it, trying to get the treasure inside it. But of course there is no treasure in the Treasury or in the other tombs. The treasure of Petra is the city itself – the city of pink stone.

3   The Serengeti migration

It is a wonderful thing to see. Every year, 1.5 million wildebeest leave their home in south Serengeti and travel north. For the next eight months, they will be away from home, always moving, travelling in a great circle. As many as half a million other animals, like zebras and gazelles, travel with them. So every year, 2 million animals move together across the flat land of East Africa.

Why do they do it? It is dangerous – every year 250,000 of the wildebeest die on the journey – but they have to do it. They are migrating – moving from place to place to find food and water. And this is the longest and largest migration in the world – the Serengeti migration.

For these animals, home is in the south, in Tanzania. From December to April, they live in south Serengeti and Ngorongoro. After the 'short' rains – one or two weeks

Wildebeest and zebra

of rain in November and December – there is lots of grass and the animals eat well.

Soon the baby animals will be born. Young zebra are born in January, and young wildebeest are born in February. All the young wildebeest, about 400,000 every year, are born during the same three weeks. Only a few minutes after they are born, they are on their feet and ready to run. And they need to run immediately. Hundreds of animals are waiting for them: big cats like lions and leopards, and hyenas too. At this time of year, there is lots of food for everyone.

In April, it is time to move. It is getting hot in the south, and there is not much grass or water. The 'long' rains are beginning in the west. They usually bring a lot of water in April and May. The animals can hear the storms, and they can smell the rain. They have eaten well for months, and they are strong. The grass is growing in the west. They know that it is time to leave.

In June, most of the animals are in the centre or west of the Serengeti. The 'long' rains usually end in May, and now it is getting dry. The best water is in the north, so the animals need to move again. Now they have to cross their first big river, the Grumeti River.

A crocodile

Often the water is not very deep, and the animals can walk across the river. They cross quickly, because they are in danger from crocodiles. They move north to Ikorongo, and there they stop and wait. This is the most dangerous place of all.

Crossing the Mara River

The animals need to get to the Masai Mara, in Kenya. There is grass and lots of water there in August and September. But first they need to cross the Mara River, which is a big, deep river. The large Nile crocodiles know that they are coming – and they are waiting for them. Day after day, the crocodiles wait in the water, and the wildebeest and other animals wait on the south side of the river. Soon there are many thousands of animals. And then, suddenly, they run into the water and begin to swim.

Animals crash into each other, and many are hurt. The crocodiles find food easily. They can live for a long time without food, but in these hot days of summer, they have the best meals of the year.

Some animals die in the river, but most of them get across. During the last weeks of summer, there is grass and water here in the north. They stay until October or November, when the storm clouds arrive in the south. The 'short' rains are ready to begin. The animals turn south, and they travel quickly. They want to be home in south Serengeti again, because new grass is growing there. They will stay there until April, when the great Serengeti migration begins again.

4   Angkor Wat

If you look at the centre of the Cambodian flag, you will see a picture of a building. It is the most famous building in Cambodia, and one of the most beautiful buildings in the world. It is called Angkor Wat.

Angkor Wat

The story of the city of Angkor is like the story of many old cities. A long time ago, Angkor was one of the largest cities in the world, and many people lived there. There were a lot of houses, which were made of wood, and many temples made of stone. But the world changed, and people moved away.

The houses fell down, but the temples did not fall down, because they were made of stone. But the forest around the city grew quickly. Trees grew up over the temples and hid them. Only one temple, Angkor Wat, could defend itself against the forest. Angkor Wat had canals full of water around it, on all four sides, and the forest could not cross the canals. The forest destroyed many of the temples in Angkor, but it did not destroy Angkor Wat.

Angkor Wat was for some time the temple and capital city of one of the old Khmer kings. From AD 802 to 1431, they were kings of the country which was later called Cambodia. We know very little about that time, because there are no old Khmer books about it. The only person who described Khmer life was a Chinese traveller, Zhou Daguan, who visited Angkor in AD 1296. He wrote about the different temples, and about the Khmer people and life in Angkor. But we still have the temples. We have learned a lot from them, because they are full of pictures.

The Khmer kings thought that they were gods, not men like other people. And because they were gods, they thought that they could never die. So the kings built large temples with pictures of their gods and of themselves. The first kings built their temples for the Hindu god Siva.

A stone picture at Angkor Wat

In about AD 1150, Angkor Wat was built by King Suryavarman the Second for another Hindu god, Vishnu. And the people who built Angkor Wat cut pictures into the stone walls of the temple. There are pictures from Hindu stories – from the *Ramayana* and the *Mahabharata* – and there are pictures of King Suryavarman and of his life in Angkor. And there are also pictures from Buddhist stories. After the death of King Suryavarman the Second, a later king changed Angkor Wat into a Buddhist temple.

But like all the temples in Angkor, it was built as a Hindu 'mountain' temple. 'Mountain' temples were built to look like Mount Meru, the home of the Hindu gods. The five towers of Angkor Wat are the five mountain tops of Mount Meru. The walls of the temple are the smaller mountains around Mount Meru. The canals around the walls are the seas around the mountains. And like a real mountain, it is hard to climb to the top of the temple at Angkor Wat.

There is a lot to see in Angkor. Angkor Wat is the most famous of the temples, but the favourite temple for many people is a few kilometres away at Ta Prohm. The trees that grew up over the temple at Ta Prohm are still there – just like they were hundreds of years ago. The kings of Angkor were rich and strong, but they have all died, and their temples will all fall down. In the end, nothing is as strong as the forest that grows around Angkor.

The temple at Ta Prohm

5   The Iguazú Falls

The south of Brazil meets the north of Argentina at the Iguazú River, called Iguaçu in Brazil. At this meeting place, the land in the north is higher than the land in the south. When the river comes to the end of the higher land, it falls off – like water that falls off the side of a table. But this table is 2.7 kilometres long, and the water falls 82 metres down its side. These waterfalls are called the Iguazú Falls.

They are not the highest waterfalls in the world, but they are some of the biggest. At dry times of the year, about 500 cubic metres of water comes down the waterfalls every second. But at wet times, from November to March, there is much more water – about 6,000 cubic metres of water every second.

The Iguazú Falls are not special just because they are big. They are special because they are wonderful to see. They are not one fall of water – there are 275 different falls along 2.7 kilometres of the river. The largest and most famous of the falls is called the Devil's Throat. The water comes into the Devil's Throat from three sides; from the top, it looks like the letter 'U'.

The best place to see it is from the Brazilian side of the river. People have built a walkway – a wooden road above the river – at the mouth of the 'U', so you can walk near to the middle of the falls. It is often wet on this walkway,

The Iguazú Falls

and not just from the rain. The falling water makes a wet cloud over the Devil's Throat for much of the year. (Visitors can borrow raincoats from the Visitor Centre!)

Most of the falls are on the Argentinian side of the river. There are long walkways on this side to many places along the waterfalls. You can take a boat to the island in the middle of the river, San Martin Island, and look up at the falls. Or you can fly over the waterfalls and look down on them.

A walkway near the falls

But it is possible to get away from the noise of the falls. On both sides of the river there are parks with wonderful flowers, trees, and rare animals like the jaguar. There are more than 350 different kinds of bird, too. And when the moon is full, there are special visits to see the waterfalls by moonlight.

But this beautiful, special place is in danger. The parks are in danger, because people want to cut down the trees to build roads, houses, and hotels. The waterfalls are in danger, too, because people want to build dams, using the river to make electricity. The Itaipu Dam – one of the largest in the world – is below the waterfalls on the Paraná River. But there are five dams above the waterfalls. The nearest, the Governor José Richa Dam, is only 20 kilometres away – and there are soon going to be more. And if we destroy the parks and waterfalls, there will not be a home for the birds and animals of the forest.

6   Chichén Itzá

There are good days to visit places, and there are bad days. Usually this is because of the weather. But for visitors to Chichén Itzá, there are two days in the year that are the best days to visit. And this is not because of the weather; it is because of the earth and the sun.

The city of Chichén Itzá was built by the Maya people of Yucatán in Mexico over a thousand years ago. The Maya were very interested in numbers and in astronomy (learning about the stars). Their buildings were beautiful, and very clever too. In Chichén Itzá there is a temple called the Pyramid of Kukulcan. On two special days every year thousands of people come to Chichén Itzá. While they watch, a large snake climbs down the pyramid, from the top to the bottom. Of course it is not a real snake – it is a snake made of sunlight and shadows.

The 'snake' at Kukulcan

It works like this. At about 3.00 in the afternoon, some of the light of the sun comes onto the steps on the north face of the pyramid. This light makes triangles on the west side of the steps – and it looks like the body of a snake that is moving. At the same time, the sun lights the stone head of the snake at the bottom of the steps. The snake god Kukulcan is coming down from his temple.

This only happens twice a year, on the days of the equinox. This is when the nights are as long as the days, around March 21 and September 22.

It is not easy to make a building like this today – but the Maya did it without computers or other help hundreds of years ago.

The Pyramid of Kukulcan also counts the days of the year. The pyramid has four faces, and there are ninety-one steps on each face. At the top, there is one more step in front of the temple. This makes 365 steps – the number of days in a year.

The Itzas were a group of Maya people, and the name Chichén Itzá means 'At the Mouth of the Well of the Itzas'. There are very few rivers in Yucatán, but there are natural wells – deep holes in the ground with water at the bottom.

Just north of the Pyramid of Kukulcan is the Sacred Well. This is a very big well. It is 60 metres across, and it is 27 metres from the top of the well down to the green water.

Now the water is still, but this was not always a quiet place. The Maya sacrificed people here – they killed them to please their gods. To do this, they threw men, women, and children into the well, and they died there.

The Sacred Well

The Maya liked to sacrifice people, and they liked sport, too. They played something like football in the Great Ball Court at Chichén Itzá. This is 166 metres long and 68 metres across, with long walls on each side that are 12 metres high. At the top of each wall, in the middle, is a stone ring with a hole in it. We think that the players had to hit the ball through the hole – but they could not use their hands or feet! It was important to win. When they finished playing, the winners sacrificed one of the losing players.

A stone ring in the Great Ball Court

7   The Grand Canyon

When you visit a mountain, you arrive at the bottom, and you look up at the mountain. But when you visit a canyon, you can often arrive at the top, and look down into the earth. And when you look down into the Grand Canyon, you look down a long way. At the bottom, which in most places is about 1.2 kilometres below you, you see the Colorado River. But when you look at the tall, red sides of the canyon, you are looking at a wonderful story – the story of how the earth was made.

The Spanish word *colorado* means 'full of colour'. This describes the Grand Canyon very well. It is not the river that is full of colour – it is the canyon itself. Its walls

are made of layers of stone – some red, some yellow, and some brown or orange. Each layer of stone lies on top of the other layers like a great sandwich.

And this is how the canyon was made – just like a sandwich. But this sandwich began nearly 2 billion years ago!

At that time, the world was a very different place. No animals lived on the land, and there were only a few in the sea. The land was different too. Where North America is now, there was a large piece of land called Laurentia. Then some new islands, made of very hard stone, pushed up out of the sea. Slowly – during about the next 200 million years – they moved across the sea. In the end, they crashed into Laurentia, and stayed there. They were the first layer – the bottom layer – of the sandwich. Now we call them the Vishnu Basement Rocks.

Layers of rock in the Grand Canyon

There are nearly forty different layers of rocks in the walls of the Grand Canyon. We usually describe them in three groups of layers: the Vishnu Basement Rocks, the Grand Canyon Supergroup Rocks, and the Layered Paleozoic Rocks (Paleozoic means 'Old Life'). The second group, the Supergroup, was even slower than the first. It took them about 700 million years to arrive. And they could not stay still. They moved around, and fell over – slowly – until the next group of rocks arrived.

The final group is the top layer in the sandwich – the flat layers of red, yellow, and brown rock. They did not move around. They stayed flat, and that is why they make interesting pictures. Everyone who visits the Grand Canyon takes pictures of these layers!

Most of this story happened under the sea – that is where many of the layers were made. And then, about 75 million years ago, something big happened. Something pushed the land up out of the sea. It made the Rocky Mountains, and it pushed the Grand Canyon three kilometres up out of the sea.

Of course it was not a canyon then. It was a piece of flat land, hard and dry, like the top of a table. But the land moved a little, and a river – the Colorado River – started to move across the land and to cut very slowly down into the rock. That was about 7 million years ago. Now the Grand Canyon is 446 kilometres long and from 6 to 29 kilometres across. And when you look at it, you are looking at the long, slow story of the earth.

The Colorado River

8 The Alhambra

The Alhambra sits on a hill above the town of Granada in the south of Spain. Behind this large red building up on the hill, you can see snow on the mountain tops of the Sierra Nevada.

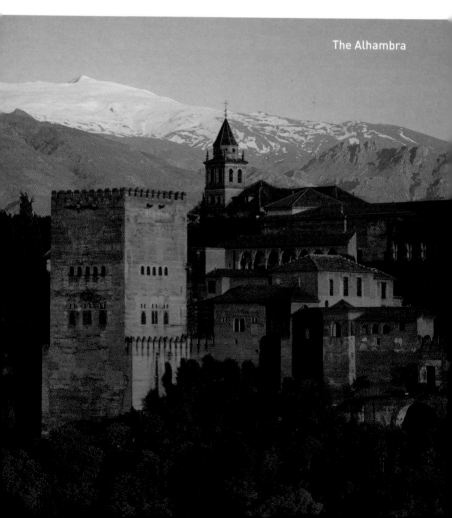

The Alhambra

From below, from the outside, it looks good. But when you leave behind the hot, noisy streets of Granada and go inside the Alhambra, it is even better. Inside the beautiful rooms and gardens of the Alhambra, it is cool – and the only noise is the quiet sound of water.

The Alhambra was built by the last Muslim kings of Spain. The first Muslim armies crossed the sea from North Africa and arrived in Spain in AD 711. In less than ten years, nearly all of Spain and some of France belonged to them. Only a small piece of the north of Spain, Asturias, was still Spanish. But the Spanish did not stop fighting. Slowly they pushed the Muslim armies back to the south. After five hundred years, only a small corner of the south-east of Spain was still in Muslim hands. And the story of the Alhambra began.

In AD 1237, Muhammad ibn al-Ahmar (Sultan Muhammad the First) made Granada his capital city. He decided to build the Alhambra on the hill above the town. He built a canal from the Darro River 8 kilometres away to bring water to the Alhambra. His new building was a fort – a place to defend. In fact, the name Alhambra means 'red fort'. It was a good place to put a fort, because up there on the hill you can see a long way. If enemies are coming, you can see them a long time before they arrive. Muhammad ibn al-Ahmar lived here until his sudden death in 1273.

But the kings who came after him changed the Alhambra. They changed it from a fort into a palace – a home for kings. And no kings lived in a more beautiful palace than the Sultans of the Alhambra!

At the centre of the palace is the famous Court of Lions. This is an outside room full of sunlight and shadow. At the centre of the court, in the sunlight, is a fountain with stone lions around it. Long, narrow canals take water across the floor to and from the fountain. Around the sides of the court are more than a hundred thin columns of stone. You can walk in the shadow of the columns and listen to the water that falls from the fountain. And you can think of the words that are on the fountain, words of the writer Ibn Zamrak:

Water and white stone look the same,
And we cannot know which of them is moving.

The Court of Lions

The Hall of the Abencerrajes

The rooms and gardens of the Alhambra are places to sit, and look, and think. In the Hall of the Abencerrajes, when you look up you see a great white star with eight arms. Light comes through the windows under the star. You think that the star is flying in the sky, not resting on the four walls of the room below it.

The Sultans of the Alhambra stayed in Granada for less than two hundred years. They left in AD 1492. But their palace on the hill is still there – one of the greatest examples of Muslim building, one of the greatest treasures of Spain, and one of the wonders of the world.

9

The lights of the aurora

On the night of 2 September 1859, the dark sky over Europe and North America was suddenly full of light. The light did not come from the sun or the moon – and it had a strange colour. The light moved across the sky, coming and going, like clouds in a strong wind. In the United States, a man in Boston was using the telegraph

to speak to a man in Portland, 160 kilometres away. They both turned off the electricity for the telegraph, but they could still speak to each other for the next two hours. The electricity was coming from the light in the sky. How was this possible? And what was this light in the sky?

The light is called the aurora. Usually you can see it only at the very north of the earth, where it is called the aurora borealis or Northern Lights, or at the very south, where it is the aurora australis or Southern Lights. But in 1859, something happened in the sun – a very large storm – and it moved the aurora across the middle of the earth. We do not think that this ever happened before 1859, and we know that it has not happened since then.

The aurora borealis (Northern Lights) over Sommarøy, Norway

The light of the aurora does not come every night. It comes because of storms 150 million kilometres away, in the sun. And the best times to see the light of the aurora are around the equinoxes, in March and September. Most often, the aurora is green, but it can be blue, or red, or any colour between. Sometimes the light is still, like the lights of a town far away; sometimes the light moves, dancing in the sky.

But why does the aurora happen? And why can we only see it at the top or bottom of the earth? The aurora is made by something called the 'solar wind' (wind from the sun). We cannot see this wind, or touch it. It is a wind of particles that travel away from the sun all the time at about 400 kilometres a second.

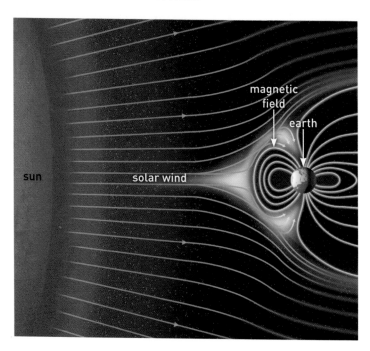

Most of the particles never touch the earth. The earth has a kind of 'wall' around it that defends it against these particles. This wall is called the earth's magnetic field, and it pushes the particles away on either side. It is like water going to each side of a large stone in a river. But the earth's magnetic field has two 'windows' in it: the magnetic north, and the magnetic south. At these places, the earth's magnetic field turns down into the earth. And some of the particles from the solar wind come through these magnetic 'windows'. These solar particles crash into the particles that are already in our sky. And when this happens, we see the beautiful lines or clouds of light of the aurora.

Where can you see the aurora? Alaska is a good place to see the aurora borealis, and you can also go to places like Iceland, Siberia, the north of Greenland, Norway, Sweden, and Scotland. To see the aurora australis, go to the south of Australia, Tasmania, or New Zealand.

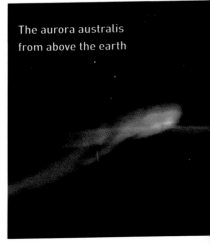

The aurora australis from above the earth

People travel thousands of kilometres to see the aurora, and they can never be sure that it will happen. But people who do see it say that they will never forget it. So if you are ready to wait in the cold, and if you are lucky, perhaps you too will see the aurora when it dances across the sky.

10   Kyoto

The name Kyoto means 'capital city'. And for more than a thousand years, from 794 until 1868, Kyoto was the capital city of Japan. For many people, it is still the most important city in the country.

But Kyoto is two cities – a new one and an old one – in one place. The new Kyoto is a busy, noisy, modern city, just like so many cities around the world. The old Kyoto is a quiet place with its gardens and its temples made of wood. And the old city is still alive. In Kyoto, the old and the new live together, hand in hand.

If you want to visit Saiho-ji, one of the old Buddhist temples, you must do more than just pay money. You must sit quietly for some time, then say or write Buddhist prayers, before you can go in. This temple has a moss garden, which was made by the famous Japanese gardener Muso Soseki in 1339. The garden is cool, green, and beautiful.

Saiho-ji

Kiyomizu-dera

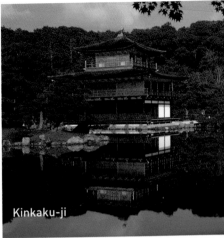
Kinkaku-ji

In old Kyoto, natural things are as important as things made by people, so the gardens are as important as the temples. If you want to see the temples at their best, then you have to see the gardens at their best. And the two best times to see the gardens are in the spring and in the autumn.

In the spring, during April, the cherry trees come into flower. This is the best time to visit Kiyomizu-dera. This wooden temple was built on the side of a hill – and it was made without any nails! The front of the temple has tall, wooden columns. You can stand here and look at the pink and white flowers of the hundreds of cherry trees. From here you can see a lot of the city of Kyoto too.

Kinkaku-ji, a beautiful gold temple, looks good at any time of year. In the spring, the cherry trees are in flower. In the autumn, the leaves on the trees change colour – they are now red, yellow, and green. And in the winter, everything is white when the snow falls.

This temple was built by Shogun Yoshimitsu to be his home in 1397, but his son changed it into a temple. Fire has destroyed the temple three times, the last time in 1950. But each time, the temple is built again – and the place is as beautiful as ever.

The 'dry' garden

The most famous garden in old Kyoto has got no flowers or trees at all. This 'dry' garden, in the temple of Ryoan-ji, is made only of stones – but it is a very important place to Buddhists. The garden is 30 metres long and 10 metres across, and it has a little wall around it. In the garden, there are fifteen large stones, with moss around them, in a bed of small white stones. Every day, the gardener of the temple makes lines in the small white stones – circles around the large stones, and lines between them. The large stones are in five groups – and it is only possible to see fourteen stones at the same time. One stone is always hiding behind the others. It is possible to see the last stone, say the Buddhists, but only after you have sat still for a very long time.

11   The Great Barrier Reef

'The largest living thing in the world' – that is how many people describe the Great Barrier Reef. And they are right, because this living thing is more than 2,500 kilometres long – and it is alive. The reef is growing all the time, because of very small sea animals called corals.

Corals are unusual animals, because they make the island that is their home. This island is not made of stone; it is made by the corals from calcium carbonate. Millions of corals together make an island under the water which

Corals

The Great Barrier Reef

is called a coral reef. And the Great Barrier Reef is a long line of about 3,000 coral reefs and 900 islands near the north-east of Australia. It is home to thousands of kinds of fish and other sea animals.

Coral reefs are good places to live. There are lots of holes, which are good places for fish to hide, and which are easy to defend. There are many dangerous fish around the reef, but there is lots of food too. There are not many coral reefs in our seas – less than 1 per cent of our seas have coral reefs in them. But our coral reefs are home to 25 per cent of all things that live in the sea.

And the important thing is this – coral reefs are beautiful places! Corals need seawater, but they also need sunlight. Because of this, corals do not usually live in deep, dark water – they prefer water that is less than 150 metres deep. So the water around a coral reef is warm, and full of light and life. Millions of visitors come to the Great Barrier Reef every year to see the beautiful reefs and sea animals.

A sea cow

Some of the sea animals on the Great Barrier Reef are very rare. One of these is the sea cow (also called the dugong). Just like cows that live on the land, the sea cow eats grass – but it is a kind of sea grass that grows under the water. It is called a 'cow', but there is another land animal that is more like it. Just look at its nose. Yes, it is the elephant!

A sea turtle

A crown-of-thorns starfish

There are seven kinds of sea turtle in the world, and six of them live on the Great Barrier Reef. The turtle is one of our oldest animals. We know that the first turtles lived more than 200 million years ago. Turtles can live for as much as eighty years. They need to live for a long time – some mother turtles do not begin to have their babies until they are twenty or even thirty years old!

The Great Barrier Reef is one of the great natural wonders of the world. But, like other coral reefs, it is in danger. One of the dangers is natural: it is an animal called the crown-of-thorns starfish, which eats corals. Is this a big danger? Fifty years ago, we thought it was, but today we are not sure. Some years there are more of these starfish, some years there are fewer. But there are also two dangers that come from people. First, the sea is getting dirtier, and second, it is getting warmer. Both of these things kill coral reefs. And both of these dangers are getting worse. Will people destroy the largest living thing in the world?

12   Qin's last army

In 1974, some workers were making a well in the ground near Xi'an in China. They were looking for water, when they hit something hard in the ground. It was the head of a soldier – not a real soldier, but a soldier made of terracotta. They took the soldier out of the ground. He was two metres tall, and he was beautifully made. And he was not alone. There were more soldiers under the ground, and horses, and weapons. The workers were looking for water, but they found an army.

The army was made more than two thousand years ago for a man called Ying Zheng – a man who changed the world. At that time, China was not one country but seven different countries. Ying Zheng's father was king of one of those countries. When he died, Ying Zheng was only thirteen, but he followed his father as king. And he started to make two armies. He made his first army to fight for him while he was alive. And he made his second army to fight for him when he was dead.

He used his first army to fight against the other six countries of China. After twenty-five years, in 221 BC, he was an emperor – a king of many countries. He changed China from seven countries into one country – the country that it still is today. And he changed his name. His new name was Qin Shi Huang Di, the First Emperor of China.

The terracotta army

But his second army was not ready yet. This army – the terracotta army – took more than thirty years to build. And he used 700,000 people to build it for him. They made more than 8,000 terracotta soldiers, each one with a different face, each one like a real person. And they gave each soldier real weapons to defend their emperor. They made horses for the soldiers to ride. They made people to play music for him, and dancers to dance for him, and birds to fly around his head. And when they were ready, the emperor put them all into the ground around his tomb.

Soldiers' faces

We know that this is true because we have found some of these things under the ground. Many of them are still under the ground. By 2010, nearly 1,900 of the soldiers were out of the ground; the rest are waiting for us to bring them out. We have found the soldiers who defend the tomb; but we have not opened the tomb itself. Not yet.

There is an old story about the tomb. About a hundred years after the death of the First Emperor in 210 BC, a man called Sima Qian wrote about the emperor and his tomb. He said that the tomb was as big as a city, with streets and houses, and an army to defend it. He said that the houses were made of gold and other kinds of treasure. For two thousand years, no one thought that his words were true. But we have found the emperor's last army. What secrets are still waiting for us in his tomb?

13 Tomorrow's wonders

Now you have read about eleven of the world's wonders – some from millions of years ago, and some from only a few hundred years ago. Of course there are hundreds of others, and everyone has their favourites.

One hundred years from now, what will the favourites be? The Millau Bridge, more than 300 metres high, in the south of France? The Palm Islands of Dubai? The statues of Easter Island? The Channel tunnel, which goes under the sea between England and France? The Three Gorges Dam in China? Or something newer still? Nobody knows. But we do know one thing: people will never stop making new and wonderful things.

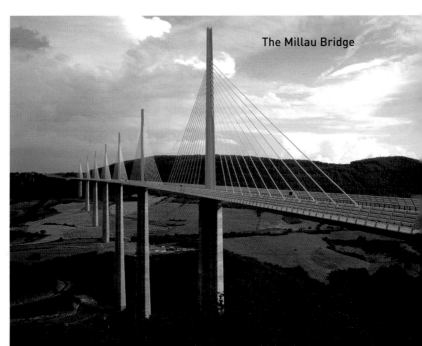

The Millau Bridge

GLOSSARY

Buddhist (*n & adj*) following the teachings of Buddha

calcium carbonate ($CaCO_3$) something solid and white that is found in chalk and some kinds of stone

camel a large animal with a long neck that carries people and things in hot dry places

canal a long narrow passage that carries water

cherry tree a tree with beautiful pink or white flowers

city a big and important town; **capital city** the most important city in a country

column a tall piece of stone or wood that is part of a building

cool a little cold; between warm and cold

cubic metre the volume of something that is 1 metre long, 1 metre wide, and 1 metre high (m^3)

dam a wall that is built across a river to hold the water back

defend to fight to keep away people or things that attack

destroy when something is destroyed, it is dead and finished (e.g. fire destroys a forest)

earth the world; the planet that we live on

earthquake a sudden strong shaking of the ground

electricity power that makes machines work and can make heat and light

elephant a very big wild animal with a long nose that hangs down

entrance the door or opening where you go into a place

flag a piece of cloth with a special pattern on it; every country has its flag

flat (*adj*) smooth, with no parts higher or lower than the rest

forest a large area of land covered with trees

gazelle a small animal like a deer that can run very fast

god a spirit that people believe has power over them and nature

grass a plant with thin green leaves that grows on the ground

grow to get bigger; (of a plant) to exist in a particular place

harbour a place where ships can stay safely in the water

Hindu belonging to the religion of Hinduism

hyena a wild animal like a dog that eats dead animals

jaguar a large wild cat with black spots

kind a group of things that are the same in some way

king the most important man in a country

land the part of the earth that is not the sea; a piece of ground

line a long thin mark like this _____

magnetic able to attract things made of iron; **magnetic field** an area with a magnetic force

moss a very small green plant that grows in wet places

Muslim following the religion of Islam

nail a thin piece of metal that holds pieces of wood together

natural made by nature, not by people

park a large place with trees and gardens where people can walk

particle a very small piece of something

pink with a light red colour

prayer words that you say to God or a god

rare not found very often

rock something very hard that is found in the ground

shadow a dark shape that something makes on the ground when it is between the sun and the ground

snake an animal with a long thin body and no legs

spice a small part of a plant that you put in food to make it taste good

sport a game like football, tennis etc.

statue a model of a person, made from stone or metal

telegraph a way of sending messages along wires using electricity

temple a building where people worship a god or gods

terracotta a red-brown earth that is cooked to make it hard

treasure something that is worth a lot of money; **treasury** a place where valuable things are kept

weapon something that you use to fight with

wildebeest a large wild animal with curved horns

zebra a wild animal like a horse with black and white stripes on its body

ACTIVITIES

Before Reading

1 Match the words to the pictures. You can use a
dictionary.

1 ☐ waterfall   2 ☐ forest   3 ☐ snake
4 ☐ temple   5 ☐ flags   6 ☐ park

2 Where are these world wonders? Circle the correct words.

The Serengeti migration is in *India / Africa*, and
the Iguazú Falls are in *South / North* America.
The Alhambra is in *Spain / Italy*, and the Great Barrier
Reef is near *Mexico / Australia*. Qin's last army is in
China / Japan, and Kyoto is in *China / Japan*.

ACTIVITIES

While Reading

Read Chapter 1. Choose the best question-word for these questions, and then answer them.

How long / What / Which / Who

1 . . . wrote about the Wonders of the Old World?
2 . . . was the Colossus at Rhodes?
3 . . . Wonder from the Old World is still here today?
4 . . . was the Great Pyramid the tallest building in the world?

Read Chapters 2 and 3. Then rewrite these untrue sentences with the correct information.

1 You can drive to the city of Petra.
2 People built the Treasury from stone two thousand years ago.
3 The Nabataeans moved water around the city in bottles.
4 Three bad earthquakes destroyed much of Petra.
5 Everybody photographs the beautiful white stone of Petra.
6 On top of the Treasury there is a stone fish.
7 Two million animals die every year on the Serengeti migration.
8 The baby animals are born before the 'short' rains.
9 The animals begin the migration in June.
10 The first river that they cross is the Mara River.
11 Wildebeest wait in the river to catch animals for food.

Read Chapters 4 and 5. Write yes (Y) or no (N) next to these sentences about Angkor Wat and the Iguazú Falls.

Angkor Wat . . .

1 . . . was built of wood.

2 . . . had water all around it.

3 . . . was built by a Hindu god.

4 . . . has five towers, like Mount Meru.

The Iguazú Falls . . .

5 . . . are between two South American countries.

6 . . . are more than three kilometres long.

7 . . . often have a cloud over them at the Devil's Throat.

8 . . . are only 20 kilometres below the Salto Caxias dam.

Read Chapters 6 and 7. Then circle *a*, *b* or *c*.

1 You can see the snake at Kukulcan _____ a year.

   a) once   b) twice   c) three times

2 There are a lot of _____ in Yucatán.

   a) waterfalls b) rivers   c) wells

3 Many Maya people _____ in the Sacred Well.

   a) died   b) swam   c) washed

4 The Maya used the Great Ball Court for _____.

   a) markets   b) sport   c) lessons

5 The winning players _____ one of the losing players.

   a) killed   b)hurt   c) shot

6 The _____ of the Grand Canyon are of many different colours.

   a) waters   b) mountains c) layers

7 People love to _____ the Layered Paleozoic Rocks.

   a) photograph b) climb   c) jump off

Read Chapter 8. Then fill in the gaps with these names.

Court of Lions, Darro, Ibn Zamrak, North Africa,
Sierra Nevada, Sultan Muhammad the First

1 The mountains near Granada are called the _____.
2 The Muslim armies arrived in Spain from _____.
3 _____ built the Alhambra as a fort.
4 Water for the Alhambra came from the _____ River.
5 There are a hundred columns around the _____.
6 The words about water and stone on the side of the
   fountain are by _____.

Read Chapters 9 and 10 and complete these sentences
with the correct words.

1 The electricity for the telegraph came from the
   wind / light in the sky.
2 The aurora is usually *green / white.*
3 The solar wind travels from *the earth to the sun /*
   the sun to the earth.
4 You can often see the aurora borealis in
   Alaska / Australia.
5 Before you visit Saiho-ji, you must *wait quietly /*
   wash yourself.
6 There are no *walls / nails* in the temple of
   Kiyomizu-dera.
7 The temple at Kinkaju-ji is the *third / fourth* temple in
   this place.
8 Most people can only see *fourteen / fifteen* stones in
   the garden at Ryoan-ji.

Read Chapter 11. Are these sentences true (T) or false (F)? Rewrite the false ones with the correct information.

1 The Great Barrier Reef is made from stone by very small animals.
2 Fish like living in coral reefs.
3 Coral reefs do not grow in the deep ocean.
4 Another name for the dugong is the sea elephant.
5 On the Great Barrier Reef you can find all the kinds of sea turtle in the world.
6 The crown-of-thorns starfish is a danger to coral reefs.
7 Corals do not grow well in dirty, warm seas.

Read Chapters 12 and 13, then answer these questions.

1 How did the workers find the first soldier?
2 What other things did they find under the ground?
3 How old was the army?
4 How old was Ying Zheng when he became king?
5 How long did he take to make the new country of China?
6 How many people worked on the terracotta army?
7 How long did they work on it?
8 How were the soldiers like real people?
9 Who wrote about the emperor and his tomb?
10 In his story, what were the houses made of?
11 What did people think about his story?
12 Which modern wonder goes from France to England?
13 Which modern wonder was built in the sea?
14 Which modern wonder will make electricity?

ACTIVITIES

After Reading

1 Use the clues below to complete this crossword with words from the story. Then find the hidden eight-letter word.

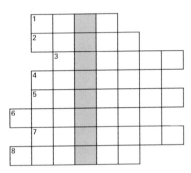

1 A big and important town.

2 A small sea animal that makes the Great Barrier Reef.

3 To fight to keep away people or things that attack.

4 A dark shape that something makes on the ground when it is between the sun and the ground.

5 To break something completely so that you cannot use it again.

6 Made by nature, not people.

7 The Great _____ is the only Wonder of the Old World that is still with us today.

8 A lot of trees growing together in one place.

The hidden word in the crossword is _____.
Where did people look for this for many years but not find it?

2 **Here are two postcards from two different wonders in this book. Complete them using the words below.**

birds / cloud / full / garden / gardener / jaguars / noisy / only / parks / pink / raincoat / same /smiled / spring / stones / temple / unusual / walkway / watch / wet

---

Hi Sam!

This is an exciting place, but it's very _____! Yesterday we went along the _____ to see the Devil's Throat. It was like walking in the middle of a _____! I wore a _____, but my shoes were _____ of water. Everybody has to shout, of course, because the falls are very _____. But they are beautiful, too. It's good to stand and _____ the waterfalls – we were there for hours. Today we went for a walk in one of the _____. There were lots of different kinds of _____ there, but I didn't see any _____. Perhaps we'll see one tonight.

Love, Emily

Hello Tom

We're enjoying our visit to Kyoto. It's true, _____ really is a good time to come. We went to Kiyomizu-dera and looked out from the _____. In front of us there was a sea of _____ and white flowers on top of the cherry trees. It was beautiful. And we visited a very famous _____ at the temple of Ryoan-ji. It was a very _____ garden for us, because it had no flowers or trees – only_____! They say that you can see all fifteen big stones at the _____ time. We looked and looked, but we could _____ see fourteen. We asked the _____ about it – but he just _____!

Bye! Jess and Hattie.

3 There is one word in each group that does not belong. Which is it? Then choose the best heading for each group from the list below.

buildings, land animals, natural things, sea animals, water

1 _____: camel, elephant, moss, wildebeest, zebra
2 _____: aurora, canal, dam, falls, harbour
3 _____: coral, dugong, jaguar, starfish, turtle
4 _____: column, fort, palace, pyramid, temple
5 _____: canyon, land, reef, rock, statue

4 Do you agree or disagree with these sentences? Why?

1 It is wrong to spend a lot of money on old Wonders, because nothing can stay on earth forever.
2 It is better to visit the wonders in your own country before you travel around the world to see others.
3 Natural wonders are not as interesting as wonders that are made by people.
4 People will be more interested in world wonders if they can see them in films and computer games.

5 Find a wonder – old or new, natural or not – that is interesting to you. Plan and give a talk about your wonder to your class. Websites like whc.unesco.org/en/list and new7wonders.com/en/index/ can help you. If you want, the class can choose the best wonder after all the talks. You could include facts about:

- where it is, and how old it is;
- why it is interesting;
- who made it, and why;
- what you can see and do there today.

ABOUT THE AUTHOR

Barnaby Newbolt has worked for many years both as a language teacher and as a publisher of language teaching books. His work has taken him to many countries around the world.

'Every place has its own story,' he says. 'It's the writer's job to find out these stories and write them down. I want my readers to share some of the excitement and pleasure I have had on my travels.'

Barnaby lives and works in Cornwall, in the far south-west of England, near the sea. In the morning, he is a writer; in the afternoon, he works either on the house that he is rebuilding, or in the garden, where he grows vegetables. In the summer, he likes to go fishing, either with a fishing rod (for small fish) or with a spear gun (for larger fish).

OXFORD BOOKWORMS LIBRARY

Classics • Crime & Mystery • Factfiles • Fantasy & Horror
Human Interest • Playscripts • Thriller & Adventure
True Stories • World Stories

The OXFORD BOOKWORMS LIBRARY provides enjoyable reading in English, with a wide range of classic and modern fiction, non-fiction, and plays. It includes original and adapted texts in seven carefully graded language stages, which take learners from beginner to advanced level. An overview is given on the next pages.

All Stage 1 titles are available as audio recordings, as well as over eighty other titles from Starter to Stage 6. All Starters and many titles at Stages 1 to 4 are specially recommended for younger learners. Every Bookworm is illustrated, and Starters and Factfiles have full-colour illustrations.

The OXFORD BOOKWORMS LIBRARY also offers extensive support. Each book contains an introduction to the story, notes about the author, a glossary, and activities. Additional resources include tests and worksheets, and answers for these and for the activities in the books. There is advice on running a class library, using audio recordings, and the many ways of using Oxford Bookworms in reading programmes. Resource materials are available on the website <www.oup.com/elt/bookworms>.

The *Oxford Bookworms Collection* is a series for advanced learners. It consists of volumes of short stories by well-known authors, both classic and modern. Texts are not abridged or adapted in any way, but carefully selected to be accessible to the advanced student.

You can find details and a full list of titles in the *Oxford Bookworms Library Catalogue* and *Oxford English Language Teaching Catalogues*, and on the website <www.oup.com/elt/bookworms>.

THE OXFORD BOOKWORMS LIBRARY
GRADING AND SAMPLE EXTRACTS

STARTER • 250 HEADWORDS

present simple – present continuous – imperative –
can/cannot, must – *going to* (future) – simple gerunds …

Her phone is ringing – but where is it?

Sally gets out of bed and looks in her bag. No phone. She looks under the bed. No phone. Then she looks behind the door. There is her phone. Sally picks up her phone and answers it. *Sally's Phone*

STAGE 1 • 400 HEADWORDS

… past simple – coordination with *and, but, or* –
subordination with *before, after, when, because, so* …

I knew him in Persia. He was a famous builder and I worked with him there. For a time I was his friend, but not for long. When he came to Paris, I came after him – I wanted to watch him. He was a very clever, very dangerous man. *The Phantom of the Opera*

STAGE 2 • 700 HEADWORDS

… present perfect – *will* (future) – *(don't) have to, must not, could* –
comparison of adjectives – simple *if* clauses – past continuous –
tag questions – *ask/tell* + infinitive …

While I was writing these words in my diary, I decided what to do. I must try to escape. I shall try to get down the wall outside. The window is high above the ground, but I have to try. I shall take some of the gold with me – if I escape, perhaps it will be helpful later. *Dracula*

STAGE 3 • 1000 HEADWORDS
… should, may – present perfect continuous – *used to* – past perfect
– causative – relative clauses – indirect statements …

Of course, it was most important that no one should see Colin, Mary, or Dickon entering the secret garden. So Colin gave orders to the gardeners that they must all keep away from that part of the garden in future. *The Secret Garden*

STAGE 4 • 1400 HEADWORDS
… past perfect continuous – passive (simple forms) –
would conditional clauses – indirect questions –
relatives with *where/when* – gerunds after prepositions/phrases …

I was glad. Now Hyde could not show his face to the world again. If he did, every honest man in London would be proud to report him to the police. *Dr Jekyll and Mr Hyde*

STAGE 5 • 1800 HEADWORDS
… future continuous – future perfect –
passive (modals, continuous forms) –
would have conditional clauses – modals + perfect infinitive …

If he had spoken Estella's name, I would have hit him. I was so angry with him, and so depressed about my future, that I could not eat the breakfast. Instead I went straight to the old house. *Great Expectations*

STAGE 6 • 2500 HEADWORDS
… passive (infinitives, gerunds) – advanced modal meanings –
clauses of concession, condition

When I stepped up to the piano, I was confident. It was as if I knew that the prodigy side of me really did exist. And when I started to play, I was so caught up in how lovely I looked that I didn't worry how I would sound. *The Joy Luck Club*

BOOKWORMS · FACTFILES · STAGE 2

Climate Change

BARNABY NEWBOLT

It's a terrible problem – or it's really not as bad as people say. There will be sudden big changes – or slower changes that we can learn to live with. It means the end for many animals, people, even whole islands – but will this happen soon, or hundreds of years from now?

What is the true story about climate change? Why is it happening, and what can we do about it? If we learn about the past, then perhaps there will be time to make changes for the future . . .

BOOKWORMS · FACTFILES · STAGE 2

Marco Polo and the Silk Road

JANET HARDY-GOULD

For a child in the great city of Venice in the thirteenth century, there could be nothing better than the stories of sailors. There were stories of strange animals, wonderful cities, sweet spices, and terrible wild deserts where a traveller could die. One young boy listened, waited, and dreamed. Perhaps one day his father and uncle would return. Perhaps he too could travel with them to great markets in faraway places. For young Marco Polo, later the greatest traveller of his time, a dangerous, exciting world was waiting . . .